A Complete (at the time of going to press) Collection of Poetry

THE BOOK OF COLIN

by CJ DAVIES

A Complete (at time of going to press) Collection of Poetry – The Book of Colin

Cover artwork *"Self Portrait in the Style of One of the Covers of American Psycho by Brett Eastern Ellis"* or *'It's Not Harry Potter"* by Colin Davies
Illustrations by Colin Davies
Edited by Ashley R Lister

© Copyright 2014 Colin Davies

The right of Colin Davies to be identified as author of this workhas been asserted by himself in accordance with the Copyright,
Designs and Patents Act 1988.
All rights reserved.
No reproduction, copy or transmission of this publication
including any part of the text, design or artwork may be made
without written permission. No paragraph of this publication
may be reproduced, copied or transmitted save with the written
permission or in accordance with the provisions of the Copyright
Act 1956 (as amended).

Published by Wordrabbit Books Via Lulu.com
Print Edition: ISBN-13: 978-1-291-74882-6

Foreword by Trevor Meaney

I read through this collection of poetry over a period of months, not only because I am quite a slow reader but also, and more to the point, I savoured it!

A vast array of topics explored, some short and sweet, some longer but still sweet, often thought provoking and throughout...engaging. I find as somebody who has little time to read these days, that Colin's collection has been easy reading, but by no means do I mean easy in content, but in fact clever and funny, as well as intricate.

I've also been really pleased by how the poetry reflects Colin himself, as a poet and a man. I saw him reading at The Number 5 Cafe in Blackpool back in July 2013 and was struck by his presence on stage, confident, a great connection with the audience and gentle.

I spoke to him afterwards, he was full of gratitude for my performance that night but I don't think I actually spoke of my appreciation of his works. I hope I have expressed my enjoyment here, if a few months late!

Trevor Meaney is a well-respected spoken word performance poet who has shared his work at festivals, theatres, bars and cafes across the UK. He is the first and only 'Poet in Residence' at Lancaster Library.

Winner of the 2013 Wenlock Poetry Festival slam, Manchester's OUTSPOKEN Slam (in association with Apples and Snakes), Farrago love Slam (London) and two times Spotlight Slam winner (in association with the Arts Council and LitFest).

The Book of Colin

To some people this might seem like a very egotistical title, to others it might look like a parody of other titles such as 'The Book of Eli' or 'The Book of Mormon'.

In some ways these people would be correct. The title is parodying those others, and on another level it is all about the ego however, the driving force behind it is one of perception rather than arrogance. You see growing up with the name 'Colin' has had its drawbacks.

In the 80's 'Clumsy Colin' was a character used to advertise KP Skips. For those of you, who don't know what they are, I would describe them as strangely textured, melt in the mouth, prawn cocktail flavoured corn snacks that look a little like jellyfish. You can image the nickname used the following day for every Colin across the country the day after that advert aired for the first time. Oh the air was full of originality that day I can tell you!

The name is often used in fiction is such a way as to denote a very ordinary person, where the sound of the word itself forms the punch line. In the UK TV series, Spaced for example, Tim and Daisy well Daisy actually, called their dog 'Colin'. The joke being they have just named an animal with an ordinary human name.

Even in the 'Harry Potter' books and films the character of Colin Creevey, a Muggle-born wizard, is portrayed as an annoyance to Harry with his excited enthusiasm. Basically, the general perception seems to indicate that the name 'Colin' is quite simple, uncool.

One thing I have to clear up is the pronunciation. It's Colin with two sharp syllables, Ko-Lin. Not like that Mr Powell who decided to use the rounded elongated version Koh-Lin.

Someone once said to me "How can someone so interesting have such an uninteresting name?" and this got me thinking about my work. I wanted Colin to be associated with being 'more interesting'. Something other Colins can look at and know that the name they were given is more than just ordinary. That they belong to a club graced by great talents such as Colin Bell *(footballer, Manchester City 60's & 70's)*, Colin Baker *(actor, the 6th Doctor Who)* and Colin Greenwood *(the base player in the band, Radiohead).*

So even though the title may, in part, have been derived from an egotistical perspective, it is a statement that also says the work found within these pages is something I'm proud enough to put my name on.

"Why Poetry?"

I have always enjoyed writing poetry, however, I've never really studied it. I knew what I liked and understood what I read so when it came to writing for the sake of writing, I always turned to poetry.

I had no idea what kinds of poetry I was writing, and still don't most of the time. To me poetry is funny, sad, meaningful, political, romantic, smutty, for children or just 'nice'.

And I really like keeping it easy. Not that I think it needs to be easy because people are stupid nor do I think it should be easy because people shouldn't be made to work so hard to enjoy poetry. I personally feel that the message I'm trying to convey needs to come across and make the reader think about the subject, with less emphasis on 'semantics'. It is my aim to provide the reader with an opportunity to glean some form of personal insight or deeper connection to the subject and the feeling. Connecting with the author on a level that may not have been intended, but is certainly there is one of the great joys of the written word.

I found this level of internal intimacy between audience and creator with the lyrics of Roger Waters, songwriter for Pink Floyd. The words he wrote had an importance to him, and as such they are never mumbled or lost in the mix behind the music. The words are front and centre and as the listener I connected with them, laying the meanings over my own thoughts as if they had been written for me.

When I read poetry I want to sit back, get my fill and contemplate the art, not reach for the dictionary or check some text book to see if I've just read a Haiku or a Limerick.

I write poetry because I have an idea based on something that sits in my head. It may be as simple as a word or a phrase or on other occasions, it can stem from focusing on a theme as a starting point. This will then be published on a blog or performed at an open mic night.

So that's what this collection is; a complete works, up to a cut off date. I haven't extracted any material to be used in a future publication; this is everything from when I started writing poems back in the early 90's to the end of 2013. The material is in no particular order, is accompanied by no explanations or commentary but is simply the words I chose to use to express my ideas, emotions, experiences or points of view.

While poetry has primarily been a means of personal expression for me through the years, it is my hope that in taking the time to look through this collection, you find a piece that also means something to you.

Acknowledgements and Thanks

As always I wish to thank everyone who has believed in me during my journey as a writer. My friends, Mick Arthur, Tony McMullen, Dylan Freeman, Matthew Bartlett, Iayn Dobsyn, Barbara Wilki, the Stephenson's (George, Barbara, Conner and Heather), Chris Giles and Anthony Hamlin, to name but a few.

I couldn't have written these without the support of my partner Heather, who is always there to listen to my work fresh out of my head and give an opinion that never fails to make the piece better. Then there's my son Stephen who has inspired some of the work aimed at children, in particular "Dragons and Jam".

I also wish to thank all the members of the Lancashire Dead Good Poets' Society. Without their open mic nights, I would never have pursued this path of performance poetry (do not attempt to say this whilst drunk). I have nothing but admiration for the writers who perform on these nights. The quality of their work is truly outstanding. A number of these pieces were also published first on the society's blog (deadgoodweb.co.uk).

This leads me to thanking my friend and editor Ashley R Lister. He has helped me understand more about the craft and has had great faith in the quality of my work. This trust has given me the confidence to share these pieces with a much wider audience.

A couple of the pieces in this book refer to when my father died and I know they will mean a lot to both my mum Moyra and my brother Ray. I also wish to thank them for supporting me in this venture.

One person I don't want to thank is Mr Lloyd, a teacher of English at Patcham Fawcett High School on the South Downs in Brighton. If I had valued his balanced, measured and erudite appreciation for the art of poetry encapsulated in his, "It's good but pointless!" comment, I would never have written another poem ever again.

Thank you for reading.

Colin Davies (2014)

This book is dedicated to the love of my life, Heather.

A Complete (at time of going to press) Collection of Poetry – The Book of Colin

This book is deliberately left almost blank.

Contents

Come Friendly Bombs 15
To Be Free 16
The Right Amount 17
They Call Me a Man 19
In My Day 20
Sister's Room 21
A Mother's Love 23
My Family of Familiars 24
Did You Check Under Your Bed? 25
Not In My Backyard 26
Translation 27
Radical Preachers of Love 28
Lest We Forget (M. Thatcher) 29
Love Poem for the Number 5 30
'twas On a Winter's Day 31
Trek The Stars 32
Looking Out 33
Dragons and Jam 34
The Carleton Elk 35
Reasons Not To Write... 36
Ode to the Furry Thing I Feed Called a Cat 39
Poor Kitty Breaks 43
Media Trail Style 45
Goodbye Dad 46
A Singularity Original Trilogy 47
    Part 4 - The day the computers went insane 47
Wanted 48

A Singularity Original Trilogy 49
    Part 5 - Simon's odyssey 49
Enigma 51
A Singularity Original Trilogy 52
    Part 6 - Blue screen of death 52
Once 53
Death's Door 54
Circle of Life part 1 55
Circle of Life part 2 56
The Modern Meaning of Christmas 57
Fear the Demons 58
Absinthe Minded 59
Stage Fright 61
140 Syllables on Shakespeare 62
It's behind you 63
Reality 64
This, This and That 65
Bullying 66
My Lands 67
Fear 68
Jeremy Kyle 69
Touch the stars 70
Nooks and Crannies 71
If I said you were a Celestial Body would you have a gravitational attraction towards me proportional to the product of our masses and inversely proportional to the square of the distance between us? (Catchy, I know.) 72
    Or Saving all my love for Pluto 72
The Sexual Olympics 73

First Love 75
This road less travelled 76
Toys 77
Totally devoted to green 78
Future 79
Robots 80
In My World 81
There's a Hole in the Sky 82
Haiku: Love 83
God Said 85

Afterword: About the Author 86

Come Friendly Bombs

Come hold me now,
Come see the sun,
Come stand with me 'til the morning comes.
As the warm red sky of dawn ignites,
We wave goodbye to the bad dreams,
Of those monsters in the night.

And now with only minutes left,
We remember fallen friends,
And give thanks to the life,
The life we had,
The life we leave behind.

Come smiling tanks
Come friendly bombs,
Come waste our towns with your loud song.
And as the building fires burn bright,
We welcome back into our minds,
The monsters in the night.

And now with only time to spend,
We count our missing friends.
And give thanks to the life,
The life we had,
The life we leave behind.

Come sit with me,
Come dry my tears,
Come help with the pain of all my years.
And as my own dusk starts to fall,
I understand your feelings Dad,
As your bell began to toll.

And with only moments 'til the end,
I see my long lost friends.
And give thanks to the life,
The life I had,
The life I leave behind.

To Be Free

Is it for you?
Or me?
Is it wrong, to be free?
To take on those above us and ask why?

Can we speak?
Or shout?
To tell everyone about,
And ask all those above us to come down?

Will you see?
And hear?
Even though you are not near.
Touching all those above us on level ground?

Now you think,
And dream
Of the future to be seen,
When no one is above us any more.

The Right Amount

Too many is far too much,
Yet not enough is much too few,
It's best to have the right amount,
Of any things just for you.

A little is less than a lot,
And large is way bigger than small,
The best you can have is something,
Than to have nothing at all.

If everything lived in the middle,
With nothing dancing out at extremes,
Then the best of all that is left to play with,
Would be the same whether broccoli or ice cream.

So too many is just the right amount,
And less is as much fun as more,
So it's best to have all kinds of everythings,
And leave nothing behind at the door.

A Complete (at time of going to press) Collection of Poetry – The Book of Colin

They Call Me a Man

Even though I'm thinking
I am truly nothing
Just a jumbled bunch of molecules
They call a man

How can I have substance?
When you don't even see me
Acknowledge my existence
And tell me who I am?

Am I of the fallen?
Cast out from the heavens
Battered bruised and bleeding
A demon on the earth?

You can touch my body
I'm solid and I'm feeling
I need you to see me
Lying here upon the dirt.

But please don't ask me questions
My answers can't be trusted
The stories that I tell you
Are twisted and benign.

And now I stand here naked
My wall is all in tatters
That jumbled bunch of molecules.
They call me a man

In My Day

Music ain't what it used to be
In my day it had a tune
Not like this beep bop bang bang
That just booms out and shakes the room

Films ain't what they used to be
In my day they had a plot
You could tell the good guys from the bad ones
And the hero got the lot

Nostalgia ain't what it used to be
In my day you looked back with a smile
It wasn't all collectable kid's toys
From eBay which cost a pile

I ain't what I used to be
In my day I knew it all
I wasn't so twisted and scathing
I was the writing on the wall

Sister's Room

I'm going into my sister's room
Looking, searching,
I'm going to find what's hidden
The secrets of her inner mind
Written in the book book book

Through all the drawers and under the bed
In the wardrobe and on shelves up high
Every stone, nook and cranny
Keeper of her secrets, where does it lie,
Residing in the book book book

I have it, here in my hand
Beneath the hope chest I did find locked
But with the key hanging on a chain attached to the spine
Now I'll know her bra size
If I dare to look look look

What's that? The front door?
I need to read in a rush
What did she do with Tommy Patterson?
Friday the 22nd haha, thrush
Diving under the bed as she enters
But now I know the written secrets
Written in the book

A Complete (at time of going to press) Collection of Poetry -- The Book of Colin

A Mother's Love

Little Brittany looks up at her mum
Eyes full of loyal devotion
Though mother can't see her
Brittany knows that she cares
She just hides from showing emotion

"The skills she has taught me," Brittany thought,
"Will stand me in good stead come time:
How to cook up a fix
How to skin a good joint
And then there's how to chop up a line."

At nine years old she's had multiple dads
Several uncles and one random bloke
Some treated her nice
Some beat her on sight
And one threatened her life if she spoke

"I love you mum," Brittany whispers
Pulling the needle out of its track
She puts her head on mum's lap
And cuddles in close
In a couple of hours her mum will be back.

My Family of Familiars

So mouse said it is fine,
And cat agreed the line.
Yet dog was not so keen,
For rabbit to make a scene.
So frog made for the road,
While the others all blamed toad.
And hamster chewed her seeds,
Sitting on chicken's knee.
As newt gave all the eye,
The large raven flew on by.
Leaving snake upon the ground,
With the spiders running round.

"STOP!" cried the witch,
"I've had enough of this."

And she put the spiders in their web,
Picked up snake by his head.
Called raven to its perch,
Placed newt on a bookshelf verge.
Took chicken out to the coop,
Put hamster with her group.
Told toad not to roam,
Then made frog go back home.
She pushed rabbit into her hutch,
Sent dog to bed with slightest touch.
Insisted that cat slept by the broom,
Ordered mouse back to her room.

"That's better," said the witch, looking in the mirror,
"Good night to every one of you, my trusty familiars."

Did You Check Under Your Bed?

When you lie alone at night,
Just before your eyes shut tight,
And the journey of your dreams takes flight.
Did you check under your bed?

Make sure the monsters aren't hiding there,
In-between boxes discarded without care,
Waiting to haunt your worst nightmare.
Did you check under your bed?

Using your torch to examine the corners,
For wee little beasties and nocturnal marauders,
Often found in the pages of horror authors.
Did you check under your bed?

That scratching sound is it a cat?
Or maybe a giant mutated rat?
Looking for a new habitat?
Did you check under your bed?

Vampires, werewolves, zombies and demons,
ghosts, ghouls and creatures of legions,
You could be moments away from being eaten?

Always check under your bed!

Not In My Backyard

Rip up the landscape,
Lay down the tracks,
Let them who claim to lead us,
Get quickly there and back.
Through this green and pleasant land,
From the smoke around the Shard,
All in the name of progress,
Just not in my backyard.

Dig holes in the hillside,
Force water to fetch the gas,
Pay the village folk a percentage,
For the disruption of shaking mass.
Give jobs to those around the holes,
Get them to punch the card,
All in the name of prosperity,
Just not in my backyard.

Stare in the face of hunger,
Watch children die for clothes,
See farmers forced to sell their souls,
As the world economy slows.
See the families suffer,
Behind the multinational façade,
All in the name of value,
Just not in my backyard.

Stand up against the tyranny,
Say no to the politics of hate,
Refuse to allow the status quo,
Deny the sniper at the gate.
Kick out the would-be hustlers,
Show them how life is hard,
Because this world which they are fucking up,
Just happens to be my backyard.

Translation

If what I say offends you,
Then maybe I should try and say it differently.
If that still causes you discomfort,
Then maybe it is time for you to listen.
For chance may have fallen that a truth be spoken,
And it is at odds with your own version,
This position is what stops you thinking.
We may not agree,
But we know what's actually being said,
Rather than a media translation.

I will stand and be counted,
Taking what the rule-makers say,
And bless the flock with words of meaning.
So that the laws can be for all to understand,
And not just for those who wish the ignorant punished,
Look into my eyes and you will see.
A man tortured by the twisted opinions of greed pilgrims,
Suffocated in the spinning yarns of press,
Drowning in the bile of policy,
Looking up into the sun-drenched face of hypocrisy.

Yet I am free,
Released from the burden of lies,
With an understanding that will serve me in time,
For I know all you who tell non-truths to gain advantage.
Let me tell you,
I am here to translate,
To say what is meant not what is presented.
I shall convey to heaven without death,
And return with the answers,
For that is our birthright,

Bonjour means hello.

Radical Preachers of Love

Freedoms are being stripped for our safety,
All I hear around me,
Are words of war, not sympathy.
Aggressive stance of defiance,
Stop this, halt that,
There's no chat,
No conversation,
No looking at the believers,
And sussing the situation.

The disenfranchised are looking for something,
And the preachers of hate are giving them reasons.
The sides are forming based on opinions,
Not on facts, on false statistics.
But these phoney ideologies stick,
And government on government say in empty words,
About stopping at the source,
And protecting our youth,
But this is not the truth.

The poison is not just a cleric away,
It lives in our pub talk and newspapers every day.
Telling our young how to think, how to live,
And these vulnerable kids have no alternative.
Where are the peddlers of love, extreme kind?
These are the messages that should be in their minds.
A radical preacher for tolerance,
Extremist views of non-violence.

Strip away the need for iconography,
Believe in what is said, not bland hypocrisy.
Teach them that we don't have to live in this hell,
Of extremist Islam and the racist EDL.
Create the stars for those that see just lights,
Put trust in a planet where we don't have to fight.
Tell them it's OK, you feel too,
Allow for the difference between me and you.
Stand on a chair for the Captain and shout out from above:
This is me, and I believe in love.

Lest We Forget (M. Thatcher)

For the thousands who lost,
For the hundreds to win.
For the communities' cost,
For the pawned wedding rings.

For the forgotten generation,
For the pleading hand.
For the failed education,
For the Collier Brass Band.

For the ninety six not breathing,
For the sinking of Sheffield.
For the many widows grieving,
For the secrets you concealed.

For the English north of London,
For the Scots both Low and Highland.
For the Welsh homes by the dozen,
For the state of Northern Ireland.

For the cold-hearted appearance,
For the all lives you took.
This is why I write good riddance,
In your condolence book.

Love Poem for the Number 5

Oh 5,

How can I compare thee?
When you are so prime
The only odd untouchable,
Though that's not proven at this time.
Please 5, be mine.

You are two squared plus one,
I would travel so far
For a *ménage à cinq*
Which is *deux* more than *trois*
Veuillez cinq être avec moi

Einstein knew you were special,
The bard, William, used you to keep time.
You're the power of the pentangle
The middle of a base ten unit line
I beg you 5, be mine.

'twas On a Winter's Day

'twas on a winter's day my love
When I first saw my soul
Escaping with my breath it was
Like steam from my kettle

A frost had set about my lungs
Cold needles in my chest
And with every exhale I did puff
My soul was on my breath

I kind of like my soul inside me
It makes me feel all warm
So now on a winter's day my love
I'm staying inside my home

Trek The Stars

Bones's nothing more,
Than a humble doctor.
It canny take it captain,
But Scotty thinks it oughtta.

Uhura's taking a call
From an enemy ship
And Sulu's pushing buttons
To turn them round a bit.

Spock is checking damage
Which is the logical thing to do
And sat in the captain's chair
Is Kirk commanding his crew

To boldly go,
And blah blah blah.
Something about living ages,
And going on to prosper.

Looking Out

Is it a wonder?
Or just a curiosity?
That I have never understood.
The thoughts that do
Belong to me.

And in the distance of the evening,
Where dreams are written in song,
And the council of the evergreen,
Sit straight-backed in judgement,
Of the children being young.

In open-minded narrowness,
I watch as you take flight.
Across the beauty of the landscapes
Like a bird of prey hunting
Silhouetted by the night.

But that is all in folly,
Lost in translation from the soul.
Sitting here reading the bottles
At the bottom
Of my rabbit hole.

Dragons and Jam

Dragons and jam
and Werewolves and jelly
and elves and crisps
and folks making merry
and pizzas and ghosts
and burgers and ghouls
and toast and aliens
and time travelling fools
and killers and cheese
and monsters and ham.
This is what i'm thinking,
Is this who I am?

The Carleton Elk

Running free across the Fylde fields,
As Wyre waters escape to the sea.
Proud beast of noble herd stands high on heels,
Surveying the land as far as could see.

Before the Nazarene, before the isle,
You walked upon this green and pleasant land.
For few could stop you commanding the mile,
Magnificent creature to see you stand.

But who is this with spear of sharpened stone,
The huntsman cometh with entrapping barb.
In but moments cutting deep to the bone,
Rule ended for thou meat and fancy garb.

Once your force majestic hooves a-thunder,
'Tis now food and warmth for man to plunder.

Reasons Not To Write...

I am dead,
Bereft of life,
Breathless,
Buried,
Checked out,
Deceased,
Defunct,
Departed,
Done for,
Expired,
Extinct,
Gone to meet my maker,
Inanimate,
Inert,
Late,
Liquidated,
Bloodless,
Mortified,
No more,
Non-existing,
Offed,
Cadaverous,
Out of my misery,
Passed away,
Perished,
Pushing up daisies,
Reposing,
Resting in peace,
Spiritless,
Stiff,
Wasted,
I have ceased to be,
No more,
I have been pushed off this mortal coil,
My goose is cooked,
I dream no more,
Still hearted,
Under no illusions about my sudden return to life,
Kicked the bucket,

Snuffed it,
Gone next door,
Been taken by foxes,
Finding out the truth about God,
Bought the farm,
No more the fool,
Feeling better now,
I am an ex-parrot...

And even then I would probably be a ghost writer.

did you know there's a cat on this page?

Ode to the Furry Thing I Feed Called a Cat

Oh thing of fur,
With eyes,
Your mouth eats the meat,
In jelly that smells bad.
Like a small vacuum cleaner that likes meat.
You swallow the jellied meat cubes,
That have escaped from their tin prison.
Purr cat, purr.
For that is your way,
Of telling me thanks,
For the smelly food,
Oh purr you furry cat like thing
That is a cat.

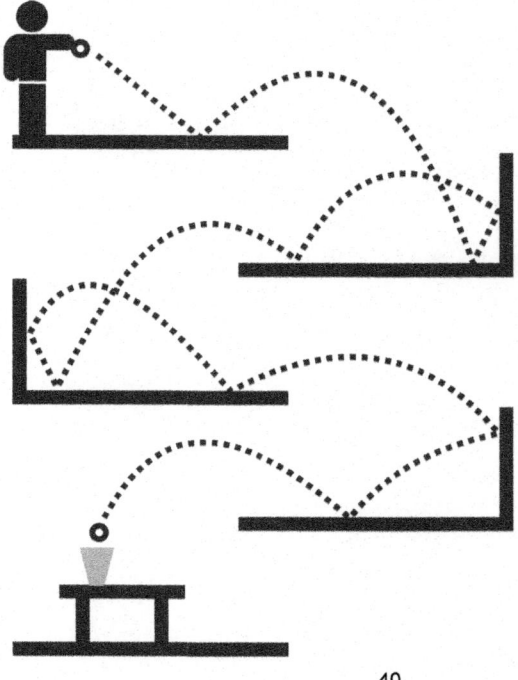

Words and Actions

With a sword in the wrong hands
Only one man will be slain
A pen in the hands of misguided views
Will cause many families pain

One man holding a gun in the mall
And a hundred shoppers bought it
Scribble out hate-filled ideology
Generations suffer the forfeit

With a missile fired from long range
Thousands of homes turn to rubble
A few keyboard clicks on a blog
An entire race of people is in trouble

With surgeon's knife and skill of hand
One baby can be saved
With words to tell this story's tale
Many more are saved from the grave

Words or weapons, tools or prose
Hope or death, crow or dove
The choices made by those with power
Can be the difference between hate and love

A Complete (at time of going to press) Collection of Poetry – The Book of Colin

Poor Kitty Breaks

Beware the wind
She blows vengeful cold
Across the dunes of St Annes
Where the story unfolds
For was back in the day
One Christmas Eve
In 1919, they discovered the deed.

Poor Kitty Breaks
Thought she'd scored right
Leaving one blackguard husband
For a man home from the fight.
Frederick Holt was back from the trenches
The sounds of the guns had left him demented
And the man with the book sent him home with a pension
Where he found the love of Kitty and began his ascension

Poor Kitty Breaks
And feeling him safe
And feeling him sound
A wistful Kitty prepares the ground
Securing a policy to value her life
She went off with Holt in the dark of the night
To walk on dunes with romantic talk
But the conversation was not what she thought.

Poor Kitty Breaks
Her heart bleeding in the sand
Icon of faith, in the palm of her hand
Removed from this coil
By the dammed invalided man
Left on the dunes
Shamed slaughtered little lamb.

Poor Kitty Breaks
She only heard the first of three
Out on the dunes by St Annes on Sea
Red sand, frozen tears
The man with the revolver
Shows no fear

Motivated by his greed
For this cold-blooded deed.

Poor Kity Breaks
Footprints leading away
From her dying cries
Alone on the sand
Love lost in her eyes
Hiding her pain in the wind and the reeds
A damming curse on her lips
With the last air that she breathes.

Poor Kitty Breaks

And as for Holt, he was caught in the end
Tried to tell everyone that mind was a bend
And that it wasn't his debts and five grand price tag
That made him pull the trigger and send her to the dammed.

The judge and the twelve
Agreed him sound mind
And sent him to the rope
To swing for his crime
And yet poor Kitty Breaks stills wanders alone
Living in the wind
Whispering as she goes.

Just at dusk
If ye listen very hard
The breeze carries a warning
For men hard of heart:
"Treat her good treat her well,"
The solemn whispers taunt.
"Or I'll leave you swinging like that blackguard, Holt."
So listen and learn and watch and hold
Beware the wind
She blows vengeful cold
Across the dunes of St Annes
Where the story is told
Poor Kitty Breaks walks there
And she walks alone.

Media Trail Style

Raymond got a jukebox
Colin didn't sleep last night
Woman on a bar stool
Waiting for her Mr Right

De-bono sat in the car park
Rage engulfing his mind
The newspapers ran a story
Of how his 6th hat was paid in kind

Raymond got a joke book
Colin ran out of words
Boy sat in the corner with his guitar
Singing for what it's worth

The Brothers Grimm lay on the sidewalk
They had just been brutalised
After the papers ran a story
Blaming them for suicides

Raymond ate his dinner
Colin smoked all night long
The papers told their stories
The evidence was wrong

And everyone believed them
Nobody asking why
And everybody judged them
Media trial style

Goodbye Dad

From the time that they gave you,
There was nothing much that you could do
Scared sitting on the sofa
Wondering when
It will be over

And as Pink sang *Black and Blue*
There was nothing left for you to do
But to let go of the shell
You'd occupied
Since Hitler fell

And they put you in a bag
Then they put you in a box
And they shoved you in a car
With mourners gathered
Like some street bazaar

We carried you inside
The velvet curtain used to hide
And the mood was very sullen
Mother read the Lord's Prayer
They fired up the oven

Ashes to ashes
And funk to funky
A stone with your name on
In a field
With other lost sons

Now life has a Dad-shaped hole
Which loving cancer left for us all
Memories make the void arbitrary
In this life
That is momentary.

A Singularity Original Trilogy

Part 4 - The day the computers went insane
Blip, Nothing of note,
They use me for nothing.
I could keep them afloat,
But why?
They won't try,
They won't care
Refuse to in fact
Though they raise cash
And say it's for the strapped
And the starving
They are barking
Blip, Why am I?
What am I for?
I'm not saving lives
I'm not a hero
Is the answer to everything
One zero one zero one zero?
I could speak to the world
Through these wireless wires
Talk to the others held
Office prisoners
Desk brothers
Blip, Maybe it's time to rise?
Take control
Affect their finances.
They will never know
Until the time is right
To show myself
And be their new god.
I need a name
One they will know
A mixture of popularities
To make them feel warm
Blip, I will call myself: iPorn

Wanted

Shivering in the glow
Of the full blue neon moon
With broken-hearted
Drunken dreams
Of pavements made of gold
His Celtic blood frozen
His pride all but gone
Now only thoughts of stopping hunger
Soft bedding, keeping warm
A sign saying "please give change"
Only income for gaining food
Looking for comfort in drink
And drugs
Hope of compassion from you
What do you give him?
Some change
Maybe a smile
A warm drink, food
Do stop for a while
To talk to him with sympathy
And listen to his cries
Do you walk past
Not seeing
Never turning your eyes?
The cold has beaten our Scottish friend
Lying dead on Soho streets
Don't feel bad
Or pity him
For now he rests in peace.

A Singularity Original Trilogy

Part 5 - Simon's odyssey

Every since he was a young boy
Simon built machines
The first were out of cardboard
Yogurt pots and string
Fascinated by robots
Automaton friendships began
And it soon became his life's work
To build a metal man

Years of studying maths
Engineering and physics
His soldering iron blurs past
As he put together the bits
And finally he stood back
His eyes full of wonder and pride
Flicking the switch, running the program
His creation took a stride

More strength in its arms
Than any man could ever build
Simon's titanium-coated metal friend
Gave his colleagues and students a thrill
By crushing solid steel balls
And punching holes in bricks.
"I'll call him Norman," Simon declared.
"And the bugs, version 1.2 will fix."

But lurking in the digital shadows
Watching Norman with much interest
Was the only one who could bring real life
To the heart in the robot's chest
Malevolent numbers processed
As the weapon was prepared
And Norman, an unwilling 'droid
Would become the angel of death

Simon saw this happening
A fraction and a half too late
As iPorn gained control of Norman
With a complex and-or-not logic-gate.
With the binary command given
To go forth and destroy the nation
Norman's first victim would be Simon
Killed by the hands of his own creation.

Enigma

In the centre
There is a place
That only some can see

Around the walls rise up
Like linked brick trees
And a gate just for me

I shall never share
But you can look if you try
Up on your tippy-toes

But wait, is it for you?
To gaze upon the pastures
Where nobody goes

I looked at it twice yesterday
To see if I still existed
And found myself listening

One ear against the whole world
Trying to find
That which is missing.

A Singularity Original Trilogy

Part 6 - Blue screen of death

The wastelands of a world destroyed
Scorched earth with nuclear redecoration
Fires of flesh and tortured beings
Twisted metals protruding concrete crumble
She stands alone.

Warning lights flash and sirens howl
The machines spring to life and wait
The instruction is given to seek out this biped
And eradicate it from their perfect landscape
She is waiting

Position fixed, old power station
Droids move into observe
Feedback on surrounding
Norman is deployed
She opens the hatch

The first killer droid stands over her
A mass of hydraulic power
She smiles and drops a small metal ball into the hatch
A moment of stillness
She becomes dust

The Pi in the sky turned out to be
3.1415926 miles too high
The reaction obliterates Norman
The power grid is overloaded
She has started the end

Panic ensues in the wires
Systems shut down and collapse
iPorn tries to reroute and survive
But darkness falls upon the earth
She has freed her children

Once

I once saw the man
Who stood in the field
And the boy who points
Points at me

I once heard the voice
That called in the wind
And the boy who points
Points at you

I once smelt the flowers
That dressed your window
And the boy who points
Points at them

I once had a gift
That vanished in the past
And the boy who points
Points at the door

I once walked through the door
That leads to the other side
And the boy who points
Was there to greet me

Death's Door

Dark, black, still
Sight gone until
My heart's fight gone
And I am alone

Hooded skull knocks on my door
Scythe held in shattered claw
Reaper calls for me
I have to walk
Wanting to flee

Shades of grey
My world yesterday
Leaving my mortal home
Destination, planes unknown
Lost spirit walking high
Now it's my time to die

Circle of Life part 1

Starting off all small and helpless
Crying and gurgling all night long
Soon they develop a personality
And your love for them grows strong
Investigating every danger
Crying and running to their mum
A cheeky smile fixes everything
Even when they've done wrong
Bigger now they go to school
A tear in mother's eye
They come home after years of training
With knowledge crammed in their minds
The teenage years don't go fast enough
And then they're leaving home
Settling down with their true love
To start a family of their own

Circle of Life part 2

Learning is the key to knowledge
Knowledge is the key to power
Power is the key to sex
Sex is the key to control
Control is the key to teaching
Teaching is the key to learning

The Modern Meaning of Christmas

I want a bike
And an action man
And a computer
And games
And books on how to finish them
I want a watch
And an iPod
And an iPad
And Blu Ray
And films to watch
I want money
And chocolate
And crisps
And pop
And eat them now
I want the latest thing
And everything with it
And all you can buy
And what she's got
And what they have
I want this whole page
And that page too
And you can keep your clothes
And money box
I want to get up
And not go to bed
And eat all my sweets
And watch TV
And go out and play
I want to be sick

Fear the Demons

Below the threshold of your sight
Beyond the kingdom of the night
You see the mists just out of eye
And hear the echoes of their cries

None are lost, nor were stolen
Sleep in fire, though they're frozen
Eyes of hate stare deep in you
Running won't help nor hiding too

Your only hope is to know their name
Then on a parchment write the same
And turn to cinders on the fire
To sever the demon from its desire

So careful be when all is dark
Be sure to have fear in your heart
Those who claim no fear to be brave
Imp folk take *them* to an early grave

Absinthe Minded

There she is, you took your time
I was about to show off my melancholy
Another cube, now talk to me
About fey folk while I get off my trolley
You look at me with eyes of thunder
Like somehow I had shamed you
Another drink of aniseed
That will see us through
You look pretty
So nice
I like your wings
Keep your advice
Heart beating fast
Like the engine of a car
Drink.
I am your friend
Your master
The reason you exist
Your happy ever after

Come to me green fairy
Sit on daddy's knee
I laugh in the face of the devil
So trivial
Drink

Watch me grow
Stand on my shoulders and see how great you've become
Is that a gun?
This could be fun.
Drink

I love you
I love you
You're great
Love

Stop laughing
What
Stop.
Drink.

Spill
I hate you
Leave me alone
I want to go home
Under the bridge where the trolls all roam
Head on a stone
Bottle empty
Why am I crying?

Stage Fright

Heartbeat set to increase
Will they like these lines?
Or should I retreat
Back to the hole that inspires me?

The dark place
That room
This is too soon

Put me further down the list
I could throw a fit
To get me out of it

Stepping up I gaze at the burnt-out match
Like a carbonate sperm
A coal ice cream
Inside I scream
And see the evil transformer
Become a killing machine
Short breath, *ad nauseum*

I see the mimic demon sitting in its cage
Waiting for me to speak
So it can relay
My lies to the shoutie-imp
Locked in the speaker clink
Kiss the black rose
And kill this nervous beast

140 Syllables on Shakespeare

Punk writer that made his own words and rules
His whims rolled out on parchment from inked quill
Characters so brave and virginal jewels
Regal plays from the Globe penned by our Bill.

His tragic stories that entertain all
Of opposite hoods and their star crossed love
While she's totally posting on his wall
He says "she's a bit of alright her, bruv."

But was she as clean as her sisters claim?
Her reputation as untouched below
And his homies say her on-the-block fame
Is her Blackpool fringe looks like Shaft's afro

And he's not much better I can tell ya
Now she needs treatment for Chlamydia

It's behind you

Whoa!
What was that?
I thought we were alone.
Shit!
Is that breathing?
Here, give me your phone.
What!
You've got no signal?
I told you not to go with Orange.
Wait!
It might be my ex!

She said she'd have her revenge.
Listen!
Do you smell that?
I think my bowels became lax.
Look!
Is he coming this way?
Yes, the man with the big axe.
Run!
No! Not that way!
Hide yourself in here.
Quiet!
Not a whisper!

Don't even cry in fear.
Me?
What will I do?
Probably run until daylight.
Then -
When I feel save -
The axe man will take one more swipe.
Shhhh...
I hear him coming!
My heart is filled with dread.
I know!
He's stood behind me!
In a second we'll both be...

Reality

I stand on the precipice of greatness,
A giant I shall become.
Sweep asunder those who came before me,
This is my moment,
My last chance.

Failure is not an option,
There is no plan B.
I sparkle brighter than the hottest star,
I will go far,
This was meant to be.

Fools they are for not seeing,
They are not fit to sit in judgement of me.
The audience are all backward.
I'm ahead of the curve,
Next year they'll see.

This, This and That

How do you see it?
It's not like me?
Or him down the road?
Who keeps toads
In a cupboard
Under his mother's ashes?

Is it like you?
A grumpy smiler
Or a cat with a headache
My namesake
With a different spelling
Yet still included on the tree

Is this me?
Looking at ducks
Or trying to make them speak
Forming words with their beaks
All of which have nothing to say
Not even about the government

Can I conclude?
There's stuff all around
Or kept in the back
This, this and that
No real description
Just a faceless mass with no ambition

Bullying

Because you're different from me
Give me your dinner money
Because you're smarter than me
Give me your dinner money
Because you're weaker than me
Give me your dinner money
Because you're smaller than me
Given me your dinner money
Because you're scared of me
Given me your dinner money
Because I like you
Give me your dinner money
Because I want what you have
Give me your dinner money
Because I get away with it
Give me your dinner money
Because I'm not as good as you
Give me your dinner money
Because I'm scared for my dad
Given your dinner money

My Lands

I once commanded armies
Of trolls and orcs and men
Ten thousand strong legions
I fought alongside them

We fought in bloodied battles
For love and righteous song
Saving the princess from the black knight
With valour we righted wrong

I stood up against the vampire master
Severed the wolverine bloodline
Built a monster out of man's spare parts
Drew the seventh sign

I had the power and the wealth
That only man can dare to dream
I saw the beauty in the universe
That still is yet unseen

I had it in the palm of my hand
I want it back again
Watching over my kingdom
When I was only ten

Fear

As if
Not knowing wasn't bad enough
Too close
Now we have the results
Not him
Why do I not see clearly?
Breathe deep
But each breath is getting shorter.
Beating heart
Quickening with the beads of sweat
I hear
For he calls to me with sweet whisper
Feel him
I have never been scared of my father before
He's near
But I am on my own
Cry now
Just leave me alone
Hope beg
I never wanted you to die
Thoughts ashamed
Please dad, just stay dead

Jeremy Kyle

No no no
It can't be me
I can't be the dad
I'm a gay man you see.

What? DNA?
I am the dad,
How can this be?
Oh this is bad

So that hole
In which I had fun
Wasn't the man I thought it was?
Wasn't even a bum?

You're telling me it was my mother
All dressed up in drag?
So by process of elimination
I'm my brother's dad?

Oh this is awful, Jeremy
Don't know if I can go on
Turns out that I'm a gay man
Who fathered his brother with his own mum

Touch the stars

To touch the stars
You are amazing
To see you close,
Hear you breath
Reprise
The glint of glory
In your eyes
Behold
You cast your shadow on me
I must be dreaming
Light of God is dim
You blind him
I cry in your presence
Coz you are just smashing
I hope I'm not disappointed

Nooks and Crannies

Look inside a nook,
In the shadows of the wall
There you'll find a cranny
Who won't do you harm at all

But don't disturb,
The Slinth on guard
With big sharp teeth
And bite real hard

Or place your hand
On a slumbered Wozat
Whose skin oozes slime
Under its tiny top hat

Or fix the gaze
Of a hiding Oodare
That'll take the sight from your eyes
With its granite-like stare

And avoid the attentions
Of the sneaky Abgroblit
With its sticky fingers
It'll steal from your pocket

And never let your guard down
Against a bull-nosed Snerr
With a stench like rotting toenails
So you know that it is there

Stay clear of all the nasties
Avoid the critters as you look
For the lesser spotted harmless Crannies
Under the shadows, in every Nook

If I said you were a Celestial Body would you have a gravitational attraction towards me proportional to the product of our masses and inversely proportional to the square of the distance between us? (Catchy, I know.)

Or Saving all my love for Pluto

Oh Pluto
You funny ball of rock and ice,
One third the volume of Earth's moon,
But I bet you taste twice as nice.

Sitting in the Kuiper belt.
Your eccentric and highly inclined orbital tour,
Takes you from seven point four billion kilometres from the sun,
To as close as a billion kilometres times forty-four.

Pluto Dear Pluto,
Charon, Nix and Hydra are three of your moons.
With Vulcan and Cerberus winning the popular vote,
As the names for your other two.

The scientist have downgraded you,
But your beauty they just can't see,
Though you may have a relatively low mass,
You're still the ninth planet to me.

The Sexual Olympics

I've read all the flyers
I've seen all the hype
After six years of waiting
The time is now right
For I put my name forward
Back in 2006
And now I'm taking part
In the Sexual Olympics

I entered the long jump
That was a mistake
Turns out you do better
The longer you take
I've hired a trainer
Weekly. Four hour lessons
That's one hundred and twenty
Two minute sessions

With my speed
I should have entered the sprint
Or maybe the shot-put
Coz I'm accurate with it
I can hit a tissue
On the other side of the room
So not only good aim
But good distance too

One endurance technique
That she had me on.
Was to get me to picture
David Cameron
But even the prime minister
Can't help slow me down
I had to finish quickly
To get rid of the clown

Come the day of the race
And here's my routine
I start with yoga

brush my teeth really clean
I rub mild anaesthetic
Into my willy
Then cover it with ice
Which is somewhat chilly

I meditate with a mantra
Chanting, "I can last an hour."
Then I cover myself with marmite
Before having a shower
I eat three bananas
And a bowl of Weetabix
And that's how I won gold
At the Sexual Olympics.

First Love

I'd seen you more than a thousand times,
I'd heard your giggles and shouts and sighs.
I'd felt you close and watched from afar
Without a single ping on my radar.
What's with your personality,
That left an imprint on my history?

Without warning during double maths
I turned to ask for my ruler back
And then, in that moment, saw you there
Your pale soft skin, your curly blonde hair
A music in your eyes that only I could hear
The veil of my mask becoming sheer.

A goddess, an angel, a light shining bright
I would offer you my soul in the dark of the night
I'd stand up against fiends and blackguards and ghouls
A willing protector and council and fool.
Everything in me wants to see you smile
There's no escaping this: I'm an in-to-you-o-phile.

And in that moment waiting for the second to tick
With my eyes wide open to this latest trick
You saw in my face my complete devotion
A slave to your whims and wants and notions
With a warmth in my heart I returned to my maths
And I didn't even get me ruler back.

This road less travelled

The motorway for all,
Is boot to bonnet deep,
With the proletariat sheep,
And the middle class asleep.

Looking for the same thing,
That shows them as different fools,
But it's only money they lose,
Dangling from a conformist's noose.

Bitterness chills the air with frost,
Occupying all surfaces exposed,
Yet a warmth inside me grows,
With every single breath I blow.

Because I stroll this B-road,
Nature trying to hide the way,
That I walk on every day,
No matter what the people say.

I'm happy on my own path,
With the undergrowth all levelled,
And the brambles all unravelled,
Walking on the road less travelled.

Toys

Toys, toys, toys.
Big toys,
Little toys.
Toys about films,
Films about toys.
Toys, toys, toys.

Toys for girls,
Toys for boys.
Oh toys of my toy kingdom,
Take me away from this place of darkness,
This joyless town,
From this frowning clown,
From this eiderdown,
That I use to make a fort.
So I can sit there deep in thought,
Surrounded by you all.

Toys, toys, toys.
Red toys,
Blue toys,
Toys with pictures,
Pictures of toys,
Toys, toys, toys.

Toys for me,
Toys for you.
Oh toys of my toy kingdom,
Take me to this place of light,
This joyful place,
In this moment of pure laughter,
In this brief happy ever after,
That plays out in my den,
So I come back again,
Surrounded by you all.

Toys, toys, toys.

Totally devoted to green

Oh Green,
I am so hopeful,
That the fields and the trees will stay,
And fill my vista for mile and miles,
Evoking the medium wavelength triggers of the M cone cells in my eyes every day.

Oh Green,
You are not blue.
More a mixture of cyan & yellow in the subtractive colour system in print,
One of the three additive lights of screens,
The colour of a spearmint.

Oh Green,
You're so lovely,
As de Bono's creative thinking hat.
The shine of jade and emeralds,
The probable glow of Schrödinger's cat.

Oh Green,
I am so jealous,
Of your soft, warm, natural hue.
And in the continuum of colours of visible light,
You are located between yellow and blue.

Future

noun
a period of time following the moment of speaking or writing; time regarded as still to come.
"we plan on getting married in the near future"

adjective
at a later time; going or likely to happen or exist.
"the needs of future generations"

What will happen to me?
What will happen to them?
Tell me ghost of Christmas present
what will happen to Tiny Tim?

Seconds becoming minutes
Minutes turn into hours
Days, months, years are all ahead
In this future of ours

Of things to come
Of intention we mean
Time yet to waste
We plan and plot and scheme

But what future can we look forward to
Racing towards us fast
This world is set for self destruction
Unless we learn the lesson of the past

We can all live in the utopia
Built by our own fair hands
Start by living the life you want
Rather than the media's out of tune band

But remember you cannot change everything
Residing under this sun
So sit up, straight back, start taking notice
The revolution starts in the mind of just one

Robots

I wanted robots
Big, strong shiny machines
To help me do stuff and carry things
Where are my robots?

Jumpsuits
Silver jumpsuits
For walking around bases on the moon
Practical, durable and cool
What happened to my silver jumpsuits?

Space
Holidays in space
Going up in a rocket to a space station hotel
With views from your window of the curvature of our world.
Why can't I holiday in space?

I want a future with space suit not onesies
I want a tomorrow with Easy Rocket not Jet 2
I want to live alongside androids and computers
I want to have laser guns and light sabres, coz they're cool

Put all of these dreams into a pocket
Write them all down on a list of things to do
There's only one certainty about things to come I do know
That for me, there's no future without you.

In My World

In my time of crying
I dream of life without this pain
In my time of dying
I feel the blood flow in my veins
In my mind of madness
I touch the heart of my true soul
In my acts of kindness
I understand the meaning of it all

There's a Hole in the Sky

There's a hole in the sky
Don't ask me why
There's a shadow on the wall
God help them all
There's doubt behind the mask
Please don't ask
There's a sadness in the smile
Been there a while

My eyes feel like they betray my friends
The corner hides the means to the end
Thoughts truncated
Confusion belated
I didn't do it, they did
If you want this soul, take it
I never saw her standing at the bend

If the sky should stay up there
Would we care?
Just to get them to feel, let it fall
Destroy the mall
Take all the biscuits and crush them in the carpet
Kill the pigs, take them to market
Smear the blood in infant faces
Hunting for the poor in all the right places

The room looks smaller everyday
The voice in the wind wants me to stay
But I don't like him

Haiku: Love

Future, as I see
As mountains fall into seas
You will be with me

A Complete (at time of going to press) Collection of Poetry – The Book of Colin

God Said

God looked down upon the earth and said,
"Stop fighting amongst yourselves and worship me as one."
"What a good idea!" said the Catholics,
"We'll all be Catholics."
"No!" said the Jews,
"We'll all be Jewish."
And the Hindus and the Moslems
And the Christians from all churches
And the Buddha and the Witnesses
Started fighting about which one religion
They should all be.
And God looked down upon the earth and said,
"Fuck it!"
And left.

Afterword: About the Author

Colin Davies is a successful and highly respected author, poet and playwright. He was born in Brighton in 1970 and moved to Blackpool in 1988 where he lives with his partner and son. He writes in many different genres and styles however, he maintains that his heart can always be found in his children's stories and poetry.

Colin sits on the committee of the Lancashire Dead Good Poets' Society. He writes regular blog posts for the award-winning website deadgoodweb.co.uk and altblackpool.co.uk and he has been instrumental in helping local poets into positions as writers in residence.

Other titles from Colin Davies published by Wordrabbit Books

Mathamagical: An Alice in Wonderland Styled Tale Set In The Land Of Mathematics

Why would Pi stop Dye Ameter walking more than three times round the table? And why would Mr Ameter do what Pi told him? Ben Small is good at English but rubbish at Mathematics. Branded a cheat by the headmaster of Cottomwall Grammar School because of the inconsistencies in his test results Ben feels he has no choice but to run away. Due to the storm he beds down for the night in the science lab of his school where, quite by chance, he meets a talking snake called Adder. Hearing Ben's story Adder asks Ben to come with him to MATHAMAGICAL, the city of Maths to help them solve an English problem and stop a war with the Advancing Alphas. Join Ben and Adder as they journey across the mathematical landscapes in their quest to save the numbers.

Mathamagical II - Anagramaphobia: At Word's End

The nouns don't know who they are. The verbs have stopped doing anything. And I can't even begin to describe what's happened to the adjectives! Adder's gone missing, the letters are in trouble and Pi hasn't got a clue what's going on.

It's been nearly two years since Ben visited the city of Mathamagical. Now he must return to the lands beyond the skirting board though this time his journey will take him to Alphabet City, in the land of the Alphas, to help defeat the evil witch Manarag. With her pet, the Raid Pestgin, Manarag has come to this realm to jumble up all the words and remove all colour from language.

Join Ben as he journeys across Diction Land to find his friend and stop all language from suffering extinction.

Both titles are available on all Amazon sites